Skilled Labour Shortages in the United Kingdom:
With Particular Reference to the Engineering Industry

by Gerry Eastwood
General Secretary,
Association of Patternmakers and Allied Craftsmen

BRITISH-NORTH AMERICAN COMMITTEE

Sponsored by
British-North American Research Association (UK)
National Planning Association (USA)
C.D. Howe Research Institute (Canada)

© British-North American Committee 1976
Short quotations with appropriate credit permissible

ISBN 902594-28-1

Published by the British-North American Committee
Printed and bound in the United Kingdom by
Contemprint Limited, London WC2

October 1976

Contents

Statement of the British-North American Committee to Accompany the Report

While public attention over the last few years in the United States, Canada and the United Kingdom has been concentrated on such matters as the causes and consequences of inflation and unemployment, a number of other significant changes have been taking place in the industrial sector. One of these is the increasingly apparent imbalance between the supply of, and demand for, skilled workers. Although the short-term effects are not so dramatic as growing numbers of jobless or rising prices these trends, if they persist, could have a very severe effect on the prosperity of our three nations.

The British-North American Committee, finding skilled labour shortages a recurring theme in its discussions, encouraged three of its members, who speak from the experience of leadership of the labour movements in their respective countries, to explore this subject and to suggest appropriate responses to any problems they foresee.

This paper by Gerry Eastwood, General Secretary of the Association of Patternmakers and Allied Craftsmen in the United Kingdom, is the first such report. Dealing with the United Kingdom, it points to a potentially very serious situation, particularly in the use being made of existing skilled craftsmen and the relatively low number of new recruits for training. According to the author, one major cause of the apparent shortage is the narrowing of income differentials between skilled and unskilled workers.

The British-North American Committee is pleased to publish this report. It does so in the hope that it will help to draw public attention to what it believes is a disturbing and worsening problem, not only in the United Kingdom but also in other industrialised countries.

Footnotes to the Statement

I would point out that there are some skills such as certain welding operations which can be taught in a period somewhat shorter than in the traditional time-served manner. While I realise that union tradition might augur against this, it is worthy of careful consideration in order to overcome the shortages of skills as expounded by Mr. Eastwood   **William L. Naumann**

While agreeing with the author's conclusions, there seems to be a mental blockage in the sections on Job Satisfaction and Job Enrichment (pages 13 and 17). The idea that high pay is a substitute for satisfaction in work is disproved by the experience of the newspaper, car and docks industries, where high pay and dissatisfaction go together. The writer treats job satisfaction as if it were a matter of maximising individual nett advantages'. But work that is boring individually can become not merely tolerable but exciting when performed as a group, especially where there is a measure of self-ownership and self-direction. It is hard to believe that the engineering industry does not lend itself to group working. In any case the notion that high pay dominates the average worker's mind is contradicted by virtually all competent observers, including Maslow, Herzberg, Elton Mayo and J. A.C. Brown. No doubt inflation distorts the perspective, but this does not make it normative.
George Goyder

Members of the Committee Signing the Statement

* See footnote to the Statement.

Preface

This paper is about the problem which appears to be with us constantly even during periods of low economic and industrial activity. As a Trade Unionist it is an attempt in a modest way to analyse the problem, the causes and possible cures. I must express my thanks to the many managers, shop stewards and workers, particularly skilled men, who expressed their views in a refreshingly honest way. Thanks are due to the members of the British-North American Committee upon whose initiative this study was undertaken. Also the Committee's Research Directors, Simon Webley and Sperry Lea whose help and encouragement is greatly appreciated. Thanks are also due to many other people in various organisations without whose help much of the statistical information would not be available.

Finally my thanks to the members and officials of my Union for their patience and understanding during many difficult periods when my services were required elsewhere.

Gerry Eastwood
Stanmore. August, 1976

Skilled Labour Shortages in the United Kingdom: With Particular Reference to the Engineering Industry

by Gerry Eastwood

Introduction

The apparent shortage of people with practical skills and the reluctance of younger people to undertake the training to obtain these skills have received little public attention. Alarmist statements are made from time to time but little has been done to put the issues into perspective. This paper has been written to draw attention to the real problems, to examine causes of shortages and to suggest ways to alleviate the situation that it finds to be a very serious one for Britain.

The paper starts by noting the simultaneous decline in British engineering output and the numbers of skilled workers in this sector or those being trained for it; it shows that the steady decrease in output is attributed by leading companies to a number of causes of which the shortage of skilled labour is consistently one of the most important.

I have concentrated on the UK engineering industry in this report for two reasons; first, concern about shortages of skilled engineering labour has been expressed repeatedly from different quarters since the early 1960s; second, this is the industry with which I am most intimately involved.

Part of the analysis is based on the results of personal meetings and interviews that took place during the course of my normal trade union duties. Approximately 22 directors, 45 managers, and 30 shop stewards from 25 different companies were seen, as well as representatives of two Industrial Training Boards and a number of Trade Associations. Companies visited were involved in some form of engineering work and covered a broad range of products —electrical engineering, marine engineering, aircraft, machine tool, car components and car manufacturing. A number of small engineering companies, mainly handling sub-contracting work were also included. In some cases no formal interview took place, so only general impressions could be made.

The paper starts by discussing the nature of the problem showing why skills are being wasted, and even lost, and looks at some of the remedial policies being adopted. Chapter II examines policies and methods for retaining skilled labour and Chapter III analyses one of the major factors leading to shortages of skilled labour: the compression of pay differentials. Chapter IV covers some longer term solutions to the problem, such as manpower planning and apprentice training.

I The Nature of the Problem

A. Problems of Definition

A fundamental problem in reporting upon shortages of skilled manpower is to define precisely what is meant by 'skilled' since this is a term that has a variety of meanings and interpretations. It is, therefore, necessary to establish a definition because a failure to do so will produce chaotic reporting and confused perception both at company and industry level.

Who are skilled workers? In one context they may be defined by length of apprenticeship training, in another by union membership, and in yet another as those receiving skilled rates of pay. The Engineering Industry Training Board Craftsmen's Category has probably the best definition of a skilled worker: 'Those employees in occupations for which a worker has usually qualified after receiving a recognised period of apprenticeship or equivalent training.'

B. Perceptions of Skilled Labour Shortages

Over the last decade there has been a steady reduction in the United Kingdom's share of world markets and a declining engineering share within it. The real output per head achieved by the UK engineering industry has been lower than that achieved by many of its competitors and has, at best, been static over the past five years. 'The Industrial Review to 1977' for mechanical engineering shows a decline in the UK's share of exports in the table of advanced industrial countries during 1963 to 1971, and that trend is continuing.

Industrial employment has declined by 16% over the same period whilst alternative job opportunities have increased by 11%. Engineering employment, as a percentage of the working population, declined from 19.5% in 1967 to 15.5% in 1974. Table 1 on page 6 sets out the number employed in the engineering industry since 1964 together with the ratio of skilled men to potentially skilled men.

Evidence that a shortage of skilled labour is a consistently important factor affecting the level of all industrial output in the United Kingdom comes from the Confederation of British Industry's Quarterly Trends Enquiry. One of the questions posed to companies was: 'What factors are likely to limit your output over the next four months?' As Table 2 shows, skilled labour shortage is consistently ranked second in importance. But as one

Table 1

British Engineering Industry Employment: Selected Data 1964-74

	ENGINEERING EMPLOYMENT *	SKILLED MEN	APPRENTICES IN TRAINING †	
	'000	'000	'000	ratio to skilled workers (1:x)
1964	4,248.7	830.3	130.2	6.4
1965	4,258.8	837.8	133.2	6.3
1966	4,411.5	856.4	132.5	6.5
1967	4,292.3	797.7	130.6	6.1
1968	4,229.0	794.3	128.3	6.2
1969	4,295.8	777.3	120.5	6.4
1970	4,315.0	801.6	112.3	7.1
1971	3,982.3	787.9	109.0	7.2
1972	3,750.8	753.8	95.5	7.9
1973	3,780.2	692.1	80.1	8.6
1974	3,816.7	687.8	72.3	9.5

* Comprising employees in metal manufacture, mechanical, instrument and electrical engineering, vehicles and metal goods.
† Data for the month of May in 'Engineering and Related Industries' Department of Employment *Gazette*. November 1975.

would expect in a deep seated recession, Table 2 also indicates much greater emphasis on 'orders and sales' as against 'shortages of skilled labour'. Because of past experiences this emphasis will reduce considerably when the industry begins to show real signs of recovery.

More specifically for engineering, the Engineering Employers' Federation (EEF) has continued to express the concern of its members over skilled labour shortages. Their 1975 survey of members [1] revealed shortages of skilled labour as one of the most important factors causing constraints over the next twelve months, with 31% placing this as the most likely cause of serious

1 *Engineering: The Continued Uncertainty*, Engineering Employers' Federation, 1975.

Table 2

The Relative Importance of Factors Limiting Output Four Months Ahead

	1973				1974				1975				1976		
	1	2	3	4	1	2	3	4	1	2	3	4	1	2	3
Orders or Sales	62	46	32	25	29	35	44	51	73	78	82	83	85	82	75
Skilled Labour	22	30	43	51	27	40	41	34	23	16	14	12	9	13	16
Other Labour	9	16	23	27	10	19	18	15	4	3	2	2	1	3	3
Plant Capacity	23	26	32	30	14	19	15	14	10	7	7	7	7	8	13
Credit or Finance	3	3	2	3	4	6	8	16	19	12	7	5	5	4	4
Materials/Components	10	20	33	49	64	58	47	36	19	10	9	8	8	7	10
Other	5	5	5	3	35*	4	4	5	2	5	3	4	4	3	5

1 = January—May
2 = April—August
3 = July—November
4 = October—February
* = power shortage

Source: CBI Industrial Trends Surveys

difficulties, the same percentage as in 1974. Late in 1974 the EEF felt sufficiently concerned to establish a Working Party on Man Power in Engineering 'to identify the main issues affecting or likely to affect the employment, development and utilisation of manpower within the industry and to recommend action to be taken.'

There is a general view, including that of the government [2], and substantiated by official statistics, that the economy in general, and engineering in particular, will suffer from the problem of skill shortages for some years to come. However, leaving aside for the moment the issue of union restrictions, there is also some evidence to support the proposition that craftsmen are being wastefully employed. Industry's perceptions of craftsmen shortages often conceal an ineffective and exaggerated demand for labour. With some notable exceptions, management structures and systems were not obviously effective and in some cases were notably inefficient. It is possible, of course, that over-manning is a consequence of companies pursuing social, rather than profit-maximising aims, especially in high unemployed areas, but none of the companies interviewed claims this and few say they would hoard skilled labour in the next trough.

C.   Training for Skills

The normal way of acquiring skills is through the apprentice training system. Although the engineering industry was deprived of a sizeable quota of its potential apprentices due to the raising of the school leaving age, it would be wrong and misleading to attach too much importance to that aspect because of the industry's indifferent recruitment record over the years. Equally it would be wrong to put too much blame on industry. Our education system is such that we do not educate for industry but more for the arts and professions. Therefore, the problem has been aggravated by a combination of the education system, rising social expectations, and the industry's poor record in security and remuneration.

Another aspect of the problem, which will have long-term effects, is that in 1975 almost half the 360 courses in England and Wales for the Higher National Diploma, the highest qualification for technicians in industry, were unable to recruit 20 students each. Altogether, 29 courses had to be cancelled because of lack of support and 31 others could not recruit even 10 students.

---

2 See for instance *Training for Vital Skills—a Consultative Document*, Department of Employment and Manpower Services Commission, June 1976.

Sir Alex Smith, Chairman of the Committee of Directors of Polytechnics stated that if the level of recruitment to Higher National Diploma Courses continues at this rate the courses face almost certain death in the next decade, with serious consequences for British Industry. He also indicated that an analysis of the diploma recruitment shows a similar pattern to that of degree recruitment. Figures are low for Science and Technology, but much higher for Business Studies, Hotel and Catering and Agriculture. Courses that failed to run in 1975 include four in Civil Engineering, five in Mechanical Engineering, four in Electrical Engineering, three in Chemistry, two in Physics and four in Mathematics. Production Engineering was one of the worst areas for recruitment, with one Polytechnic recruiting only one student.

The problem, however, starts even earlier. Parents and teachers find difficulty in suggesting to school children that a skilled occupation is a rewarding career. Young people look for work that will be both interesting and well-paid. In 1976, a 16 year old apprentice is paid £17.85 per week in his first year (42½% of the full craft rate). This compares with a weekly wage of £17.00 for a junior manual worker aged 16 who is not going through any form of training. Workers in this latter category also have the opportunity, generally denied to the apprentice, of supplementing their basic rates by working on piece work and bonus systems and can also go onto semi-skilled rates at 18 years of age.

D. The Reported Nature of Shortages and Causes of Waste and Lost Skills

At the companies visited, management were invited to give their views as to whether the shortages they perceived were primarily due to difficulties of recruitment, retention, or inadequate labour utilisation. The great majority said they experienced a recruitment problem, that the skilled workers were not on the market, and that apprentices were not coming forward. There is official statistical evidence to support their view but no comparable official evidence on the relative importance of retention or utilisation. There is a long tradition within the industry of going into the market and endeavouring to find skilled workers.

The companies interviewed were also invited to give their perceptions of the extent, nature, causes and effects of their own craftsmen shortage and to explain the remedial policies they had employed to cope with these problems. Shortages were reported to have imposed direct constraints on production varying from lost orders to delayed deliveries.

It is very difficult indeed to be objective in reporting how skills are being wasted. Some companies claimed·a satisfactory utilisa-tion of skills but this varied according to labour availability and the level of industrial activity. Union attitudes were blamed for restrictive practices, but in some cases it was understandable because of various companies' employment record. According to one shop steward it was not 'restrictive practices' but 'protective practices'. There is nothing original in that statement, but it nevertheless commands a great deal of support. The installation of numerically controlled (NC) machines is a very controversial area which gets a different response from one company to another.

When one company first introduced NC machines, it allocated its highest 'time-served' [3] machinists on the principle 'the best machine deserves the best man'. This policy did not work. Within a very short period of time the men were asking for something useful to do. The instances were high where time-served men were employed on repetitive machining work. If this practice is prevalent on a national scale, it amounts to a considerable wastage of skill.

During the 1974-76 recession, there was strong evidence to show that many companies retained as many of their skilled men as possible. Motor manufacturing and the machine tool industry are cases in point. In previous recessions the 'shake-out' was not confined to unskilled and semi-skilled, and many skilled men who were made redundant were lost to the industry. When the upturn came, particularly in 1972/73 companies went into the *skilled labour* market and found little response.

Some employers indicated that overmanning is as much an indication of weak management as it is of strong unions. There must therefore be grave doubts about the organising capability of many companies, which is evidenced by a lack of energy in introducing and pursuing policies designed to minimise demand for craftsmen. In some cases there is no doubt that given union co-operation, management would be more effective in redeploying skilled labour. In other cases management has that co-operation and still wastes skills; some treat union attitudes as given and do not try to gain co-operation. In still other cases, employers see it

---

3 A 'time-served' man is one who has served a full apprenticeship.

as part of their management function to obtain co-operation; a few have remarkable success.

E. Some Reactions to the Problems

There are several means by which a company can adjust downward its effective demand for skilled labour in response to a shortage. Some companies gave specific examples of ways in which they had designed out skills such as machining and welding in direct response to a perceived labour shortage.

On the shopfloor itself, where changes are more visible, companies have been less adventurous. Where new machinery has been installed it has been of the conventional type, laid out in the traditional manner. There were obviously great potential savings to be made here as there are in diverting the employment of skilled men from semi-skilled, routine machine-operator work.

One method of overcoming shortages of skilled labour is to utilise the skills that are available in an optimal way. It has been suggested by the Engineering Employers' Federation that employers and unions should consider jointly the changes that will be necessary to improve utilisation of manpower by introducing better production methods, including giving greater attention to production requirements in the design of machinery and other equipment. By joint agreement with management and unions, one tries to ensure that one does not send a lad on a man's errand nor take a sledgehammer to crack a nut.

Another way to reduce the demands on scarce craftsmen within the company is to 'export' the demand to the external market by sub-contracting. The problem here is that this does nothing directly to minimise total demands except insofar as the cost and inconvenience provokes companies into looking anew at savings which could be made internally. Hardly any of the companies interviewed had experienced a situation in which sub-contractors were stretched to the point at which they had to refuse orders or delay deliveries. There thus appeared to be no shortages in the sub-contracting industry, which seems to be able to take whatever work there is available and at the same time give quality and meet delivery dates. Over the years this particular section of the industry has grown quite substantially.

Table 3

Distribution of Craftsmen in Different Sized UK
Engineering Firms: 1966/67 and 1973/74

Firms employing	1966/67		1973/74		Change	
	'000	% total	'000	% total	'000	%
1-99	143	20	150	25	+ 7	+ 5
100-999	225	31	194	33	—31	—14
1,000 or more	350	49	251	42	—99	—28
All Firms	718	100	595	100	—123	—17

Source: *The Craftsmen in Engineering,* Engineering Industry Training Board, 1975.

Table 3 shows that the smaller firms' employment of skilled labour grew over the seven year period. They have been attracting craftsmen from the bigger firms largely because of smaller working units, higher wages, and particularly in the sub-contracting sector, a greater variance of work. This makes life extremely difficult for the larger companies who have usually provided the training for those workers. The reaction of some large companies has been to reduce their level of apprentice intake.

II Retention of Skilled Labour

In the view of the majority of companies interviewed, the shortages problem was assumed to be primarily one of recruitment rather than of utilisation or retention. Employers are now paying more attention to internal labour markets as a source of skilled labour, and the emphasis is increasingly on retention of skills. To retain skilled labour, employers are having to consider those factors which skilled employees consider important. These include:

A. Job Satisfaction

Job satisfaction is a function of a complex series of factors, but workers will always tend to maximise their individual net advantages. If that maximising activity conflicts with pursuing a skill in which they have invested, in an industry in which they have been traditionally employed, then they are likely to abandon the skill and probably the industry.

In 1975 the Manpower Services Committee and the National Economic Development Office formed a committee to study the Supply and Utilisation of Skilled Engineering Manpower. Part of its work was to interview skilled workers who had left the industry and determine the reasons why. It is interesting to note that some toolmakers, especially the younger ones, complained of the boredom and repetitive nature of their work. [4]

A young toolmaker, aged 22, stated that after his apprenticeship 'I quickly became disillusioned with my trade due to lack of variety'. One toolmaker of twenty years standing made an interesting point: 'Quite a lot of people leave the trade because of lack of interest which is caused by more repetitive work which is due to toolrooms becoming more mechanised'. This tends to confirm the views expressed by many people employed in certain sections of engineering where technological change has taken place. Consequently certain skills have diminished.

After discussions with many shop stewards, it was evident that job satisfaction did not play such an important role as many people outside industry would lead us to believe. It is unfortunate, but a fact, that it is now a question of economics. The financial rewards from a dissatisfying job are more important than the non-financial disadvantages, though there are exceptions, including a large group who have various reasons such as age, long service,

---

4 Report to be published late in 1976.

or location as their incentives to stay put unless they are forced out. It is a matter of opinion whether job satisfaction is a contributory factor, so one must not fall into the trap of overstating it.

B. Job Security

Another view of shop stewards, when asked to explain dissatisfaction within the industry, was that the skilled craftsmen no longer has the security which he had formerly. Security in the job went a long way towards off-setting the lack of opportunities for advancement and the high degree of control exerted over him by the discipline of the job itself as well as by close managerial supervision. Most craftsmen have invested four, five or even seven years in training at considerable cost to themselves. It is hardly an exaggeration to suggest that an employer could, in the past, do almost anything to him—give him low wages, low status, poor opportunities for promotion, and boring or exacting work to do—so long as he provided the worker security of tenure over what he considered to be his job-property rights.

With a younger and more mobile labour force, once the employer 'shakes them out' they will look over the fence to see if the grass is greener there, and other factors, pay, conditions, etc, will assume greater importance in relation to job security. If his skill can be considered an expendable commodity by the industry, then he can reasonably, if reluctantly, consider it expendable for himself. He need feel under no obligation to transfer his skills within the industry or to wait until the industry feels able to require them again. This is the root cause of so much bitterness in the industry today; it manifests itself in restrictive practices —such as refusal to make flexible agreements, refusal to accept government training centre trainees, and a host of other factors which contribute to the sub-optimal utilisation of manpower which, in turn, appear as labour shortages.

The issue of job security is one in which the industry has a poor record; 'hire and fire' has too easily been the policy. There is no doubt that security is very important, and invariably the point is made when one discusses the subject with people who have left the industry. For example, one skilled man aged 41 who had been made redundant and had 'another near miss' became a self-employed haulage man after many years in engineering 'to give more security to the family'. There is considerable evidence to show that many tolerated being made redundant and then returned to the industry but eventually they gave it up and obtained more menial employment with considerably more security.

One company which had given no opportunities for craft training until four years ago complained that the unions would not offer a dilution package. One trade union leader stated "Arguments raised against the acceptance of newly trained workers will continue for as long as workers fear that their jobs are threatened". In many instances it is not surprising that unions are not flexible on dilution agreements but if one looks at the industry as a whole there are a considerable number of 'dilutees' employed. It is estimated that about six percent have entered the industry under a dilutee agreement. Such an agreement between an employers' association and a trade union permits someone who has not received a full craft training to do the job of a skilled craftsman, subject to certain conditions to safeguard the fully trained craftsman in the event of redundancy. Such agreements were concluded during the Second World War in order to meet the shortages of skilled labour and are still extant, though not everywhere enforced.

There are signs that the industry is taking an interest in job security, but under pressure. The Engineering Employers' Federation recently told member firms that one of the most frequent and damaging causes of employer/employee unrest concerns security of employment, though the association with labour shortages was not made. Nevertheless, few of the firms undertook even the simplest forms of manpower planning that could help to alleviate the position by ensuring that they do not too hurriedly take on skilled men who will soon have to be made redundant. Indeed many, argued that it is the very existence of the trade cycle that makes planning impossible.

Some companies regarded manpower planning as research and development in human capital; for others it is 'pie in the sky' or 'crystal gazing'. In some cases it was perhaps unreasonable to expect companies to have manpower forecasts for six months or more ahead. There is no doubt that manpower planning is extremely difficult because of the trade cycle, but it is a complete deception to pretend that you can plan anything in a vacuum. Without a government policy of growth for the industry, companies will find themselves indulging in useless exercises.

The demand for job security by skilled men is insistent and companies are generally ill-equipped to meet it. Conspicuous failure to do so in the recent past has been seen to have serious consequences in at least one area.

A series of redundancies in machine tool and other engineering sectors appears to have had this paradoxical effect: the more men made redundant, the fewer there are available in the market. When a machine tool company closed with the loss of 900 jobs, another company could only recruit five; most appear to have been lost to the industry forever. For instance, approximately 60% of the Manchester Airport baggage handlers are skilled engineering craftsmen. That may be an extreme example, but a similar situation has developed at Gatwick Airport, Sussex. In the last few years this airport has become considerably larger and is still growing, with the result that the labour force requirements are such that many skilled men in that particular 'catchment' area have abandoned their skill to obtain employment, one of the principle reasons being better prospects of job security.

C. Levels of Pay

Academic research is divided on the question of whether there is a link between low wages and high labour turnover. Enquiries reveal wide variations in pay levels between companies; also general relationship between earnings and labour shortages. Most shop stewards, but few management, bring pay up at discussions. Certainly, the overall average earnings of engineering craftsmen do not appear over-generous relative to average earnings of all male manual workers—a point noted seven years ago by the Prices and Incomes Board. However, no firm quantitive conclusions of the effect on supply of skilled labour to the companies can be drawn. It is evident that the highest paying companies, with a specific policy of being the district leader, do reap certain advantages. They are able to be more selective than others and have considerably more applicants for jobs.

Methods of payment can cause serious problems, particularly in the case of apprentices completing their time and going onto incentive systems. In one company the argument was forcefully put that general machining training does not prepare apprentices to move onto certain machines at the age of 20, so that in addition to being apprehensive of the machines, they feel that their inability to cash in on bonus systems will not allow them to earn a reasonable wage. Not surprisingly, they leave the industry. Several times strong objections were made that bonus schemes are not appropriate for particular craftsmen. In one company there was a chaotic 'system' where machinists were on an incredibly loose payment-by-results method while fitters were on time rates. The firm was losing fitters but not changing the system!

Perhaps the most serious problem in the area of pay levels is the one of differentials, and this is considered in Chapter III.

D. Status

Though the issue of status does not yet figure heavily in factors affecting the shortage of craftsmen, there are indications of increasing pressure from trade unionists for recognition of status. In some companies stewards strongly express a demand for 'staff' status on questions of pension and sickness entitlements and other amenities. The comparison is not with lesser-skilled manual employees but with white-collar workers. It is difficult to assess the practical turnover effects directly resulting from this particular factor, but there is no doubt that separate status materially contributes to conflict in management/employee relationships. Nor can there be much doubt on the evidence available that the demand for status will intensify, particularly amongst the age groups that are crucial to the turnover problem. The argument for staff status is also used by skilled men to opt out of the restrictive wage structures in which they find themselves.

Evidence to show that the importance of status is increasing is contained in a survey published in 1976 by the British Institute of Management [5]. This referred to the slow progress made by manual workers towards 'staff status'. There has been considerable interest shown by some employers and sections of workers in staff status because they think it is the only logical way of improving labour relations. The survey, covering more than 300 companies, showed that since 1970, 70% of companies have reduced differentials in some conditions of employment. Skilled workers have gained more than semi-skilled and unskilled categories, and the harmonisation has been most common in those employment conditions that are given a high priority by employees—for example, pensions, death in service benefits, sick pay and holiday entitlements. One of the main drawbacks to further advancement in harmonisation is the considerable additional cost involved. Still the movement towards single status will increase, particularly among skilled workers because they see it as a means of releasing them from the shackles of restrictive wage structures achieving what they consider to be their rightful place in industry.

E. Job Enrichment

One popular solution to labour retention difficulties is to introduce a scheme to 'enrich' each task in an organisation.

---

5 Murles and Grist, *Towards Single Status:* Management Survey Report No. 30, British Institute of Management, 1976.

Industry is not normally sympathetic to ideas of behavioural scientists and the question of job enrichment is no exception. It is the factor which gets most attention from academics and least interest from the people actually involved. One company which has large numbers of 'time-served' men on semi-skilled work strongly believes that if you pay enough cash, you can buy off boredom. A personnel director argued that enrichment is only necessary if there is an error in matching men to jobs. The managing director of one company said that skilled men prefer some laxness in their work and, like civil servants, do not want to be stretched the whole time. This is the general view of the shop stewards who could be persuaded to discuss it, though academics warn, that managers and workers who are foolish enough to make this very tantalising assertion do not know what they are talking about. For most stewards, engineering work is a necessary means to an end, and not an end in itself; dissatisfied with the degree of responsibility already involved in their work, compared with the rewards of others, they are totally disinterested in a concept that might involve them in more.

F. Industrial Relations

Academic research has consistently revealed a correlation between labour turnover and industrial unrest. The engineering industry is one that has had a fair share of friction; it has given rise to the first national employers' association in the United Kingdom. The question of industrial relations efficiency and its importance to company strategy cannot be thoroughly argued here; there is a considerable body of literature[6] arguing its paramount importance.

In a situation of skill shortages, harmony between management and unions can make a vast difference. Many examples can be given to demonstrate how managements who are cognisant of workers', (and their own), interests on the questions of security, pay, status and working conditions will, through the medium of good industrial relations understanding, receive quid pro quo's in the form of union acceptance of flexible working practices and dilution arrangements. It is no accident that companies setting a good example to the industry, with a good record in recruitment and retention, have sound industrial relations policies.

Companies, of course, have to work within national- or district-level union policies, and some of them face varying degrees

6 For instance in reports of the Royal Commission on Industrial Relations.

of externally-imposed, non-negotiable restrictions on manning, dilution and flexible working practices which have some effect upon their craftsmen shortages situation.

As in other industries wages in engineering have been raised rapidly, though this will not ease the short-term shortages situation, but the insecurity, the central importance of which has been stressed, remains. On the supply side, changes in the nature of the work have made it more attractive to school-leavers. In addition, government training policies are providing an increasing number of suitably skilled people, since this is a trade that takes less time to learn than some others. On the demand side, significant mechanisation and design changes are being introduced in an attempt to reach some form of balance. Just as the companies see their best ever prospects being jeopardised, so does the union. Both therefore face a common problem without the necessary machinery to solve it. It is worth remembering that given a credible assurance that large-scale redundancies will not result, a number of unions have been flexible in shortage situations in the past and that this is not, therefore, the lost cause that it may appear to some companies.

Summing up

Companies' experiences and information provided by the National Economic Development Office and the Department of Employment, gives some guidance as to how part of the shortages problem can be eased. In particular, there is a need to pay attention to the problems arising from relatively low pay differentials within the industry, and job security. These problems have contributed to shortages for many companies, although it is very difficult to quantify their extent. They also impinge particularly upon the younger skilled workers in the industry, who are becoming increasingly mobile. The wholesale shakeouts predicted to take place during the recession have not so far materialised to the extent anticipated but if they do, they will have serious consequences for the age structure of the industry. Most companies and workers have not yet come to grips with the question of status, but there is strong evidence to support the view that it will assume greater importance between the supply and demand sides of the internal market. Therefore, the manner in which the status issue is handled could contribute quite significantly towards solving or exacerbating shortages' problems.

III Pay Differentials

It has been suggested in recent discussions of shortages of skilled labour in engineering industries that they could be caused at least in part by the erosion of pay differentials in the industry. There are three basic questions involved in this issue. First, how much have the differentials in earnings between skilled and other workers in engineering narrowed over the years and second, have they had the effect of making it a less attractive industry in which to learn and follow a skilled trade? Third, are such differentials large enough to retain skilled labour?

The main source of information on average earnings of skilled workers in the engineering industry, is the 'Survey of the Earnings of Manual Men, by Occupations, in the Engineering, Shipbuilding and Chemical Industries', conducted by the Department of Employment each June since 1963. From it, the overall earnings of skilled and semi-skilled workers in various categories can be compared with the earnings of labourers.

A. Trends in Earnings

Table A in the Statistical Annex to this chapter shows the differential of average hourly earnings, excluding overtime premium, of skilled and semi-skilled adult male manual workers in engineering from those of adult male labourers in June of each year from 1963 to 1975. Part 1 covers timeworkers and Part 2 payment-by-results workers. In general the earnings of skilled engineering workers relative to labourers reached a peak during the second half of the 1960s. This has been followed by a steady and significant decline in the relativities.

The decline in relative earnings has been greater for payment-by-results workers than for timeworkers. This is because there has been a general trend away from payment-by-results working. On average, skilled payment-by-results workers had hourly earnings which were 52% greater than payment-by-results labourers in 1967; by 1975 they were only 32% greater, a cut of almost two-fifths in the skill differential. Skilled timeworkers had earnings that were 45% greater than timeworker-labourers in 1967; by 1975 they also were only 32% greater, a cut of almost one-third in the skill differential.

Within engineering industries, structures and methods of production differ substantially. In Table B the tendency shown appears to be that earnings of skilled workers relative to labourers reached a peak in 1967 and was followed by a decline, in general, in each engineering industry, although it was more pronounced in some cases than in others, particularly amongst payment-by-results workers. In motor vehicle manufacturing the ratio of average hourly earnings (excluding overtime) of skilled workers to labourers reduced from 66% in 1967 to 31% in 1975. This is an industry in which there have been definite attempts to reduce the amount of payment-by-results working. Table B also shows the improvement in the earnings of semi-skilled timeworkers relative to labourers. This is because of an improvement in relativities in the motor vehicle manufacturing industry.

Table C shows the ratio of the earnings of skilled to semi-skilled workers in selected engineering industries for each of the four years shown in Table B. This shows that, with the exception of payment-by-results workers in motor vehicle manufacturing, the earnings of skilled workers relative to semi-skilled roughly halved between 1967 and 1975, except for motors, in which it virtually disappeared. In all cases the decline was continual year by year, until some slight reversal in 1974 or 1975.

Chart I plots data contained in surveys conducted by the Engineering Employers' Federation and the Department of Employment. The EEF survey began in 1914 and ended in 1968 while the D of E survey began in 1963. Although the two series overlap the results were reasonably consistent. It will be seen that for 1975 the percentage differential is only 29%. On this basis the relative earnings of fitters to labourers are now at the same level as they were in the late 1940s and early 1950s at which time they were at their lowest point since 1914.

Table D examines, within broad industry groupings, the decline which has taken place in skill differentials in the 1970s, for all occupations included in this survey. Part 1 is concerned with timeworkers and shows, for example, that although 'skilled maintenance fitters' suffered one of the smallest compressions of differentials, the impact was very different in motors than in electrical engineering, where it actually widened. In electrical engineering the overall compression of differentials was well below the average for engineering, in fact patternmakers, moulders, platers and similar workers suffered serious cuts.

Part 2 is a similar analysis for payment-by-results workers. As is to be expected, the changes are not as sharp as for timeworkers, though there are some cases where the differential has been halved—moulders in mechanical engineering, and patternmakers in aircraft and motors. For five of the nine occupations for which a complete comparison is possible, the skill differential in mechanical engineering was lowest.

B. Some Conclusions

It can be seen clearly from information available on the earnings, both including and excluding overtime, of skilled and unskilled employees that in the engineering industry there has been a narrowing of the differentials between the pay of skilled and semi-skilled and unskilled workers. In general terms the trends were similar in each branch of the engineering industry. By June 1975, the differentials between the earnings of skilled and unskilled employees were about as low as they were in the late 1940s and early 1950s during which time these differentials were at their lowest in this century.

The differential between the average hourly earnings, excluding overtime premium, of all skilled workers and all labourers in the engineering industries in June 1975 was about 33% (which was greater than the differential in weekly terms —31%— because labourers on average work longer hours than skilled workers). Because of the effects of the progressive tax and social security payments systems, the differential in take-home pay has been even further reduced.

C. Some Implications

The effect that differentials have on the skilled shortage position both in the immediate and long-term should not be under-estimated. In the recent compression of skill differentials, important contributory factors have been trade union bargaining policies designed to improve the position of the low paid and incomes policies based upon flat-rate increases. The 1975 incomes policy is of that nature and is expected to erode differentials by a further 3%. Mr. John Dent, President of the Engineering Employers' Federation said recently: "The first phase of the incomes policy expires in July 1976 and one of the crucial problems now facing government and industry is to decide what is to replace it. There can be no doubt that there must be another and more stringent phase. A major consideration is that under the existing policy time differentials have been so eroded that the rewards for skill have been diminished seriously. I hope that the next phase of the policy can take account of this situation." [7] Subsequently the pay guidelines 1976/1977 [8] have been published and accepted by the unions at the TUC Special Congress on 16 June 1976. Once again the restrictions on earnings make little

---

7 In a speech to the General Council of the Engineering Employers' Federation, February 1976.

8 *The Attack on Inflation, The Second Year*, Cmnd. 6507, HMSO, 1976.

or no difference to the continuing erosion· of differentials. It is worth noting that a number of unions who opposed the guidelines represent not only skilled craftsmen but people in the higher echelons of management, an area in which differentials in pay and conditions have also been seriously eroded.

In considering the relative position of skilled workers, it is interesting to relate some of the comments made by skilled men who have left their employment in a survey of ex-patternmakers carried out by the NEDO [9]. *The most common complaint was the decline in pay differentials between skilled an unskilled workers.* One had found better money and prospects working in a Woolworths Store; another spoke for many when he said "I have left because I can earn more money in a semi-skilled job". Other comments were: selling car parts and earning almost twice as much as patternmaking; poor financial rewards for skilled responsibility; my present job brings no worries, needs two weeks training and pays twice as much.

Although the survey did not enable firm conclusions to be drawn relating to all engineering craftsmen it certainly provided adequate information to suggest that many of the comments made are relevant and common to other skilled occupations.

9 MSC/NEDO Committee on Supply and Utilisation of Skilled Engineering Manpower (Postal Survey of Expatternmakers), 1975.

Statistical Annex to Chapter III

Table A

Index of Hourly Earnings Differentials: [1]
Semi-Skilled and Skilled Adult Male Workers in Selected Occupations over Labourers in Engineering

Labourers' Earnings = 100

1. TIMEWORKERS

Classes of workers	1963	1964	1965	1966	1967	1968	1969	1970	1971	1972	1973	1974	1975
Fitters (Skilled—other than toolroom and maintenance)	137	138	136	138	138	137	139	139	140	140	135	132	128
Turners and machinemen (other than toolroom and maintenance)													
—rated at or above fitter's rate	141	141	139	141	141	140	140	139	140	138	136	137	131
—rated below fitter's rate	118	116	116	121	124	125	124	124	127	132	144	136	122
Toolroom fitters and turners	161	162	161	162	162	160	159	158	156	150	145	144	138
Maintenance men (skilled)													
—skilled maintenance fitters	142	143	143	144	144	143	144	143	142	139	137	138	133
—skilled maintenance electricians	143	144	146	148	147	149	149	148	149	144	142	141	138
—other skilled maintenance classes	142	143	141	142	142	141	141	144	147	143	140	138	134
Patternmakers	149	153	151	154	153	151	154	150	149	146	143	139	134
Sheet metal workers (skilled)	140	141	140	142	142	141	143	138	138	134	132	133	126
Moulders (loose pattern-skilled)	134	133	130	134	133	133	133	131	126	122	121	125	118
Platers, riveters, caulkers	127	124	129	134	138	136	135	142	131	123	123	127	131
All skilled grades	143	144	143	145	145	144	144	144	144	141	137	136	132
All semi-skilled grades	126	127	124	124	122	122	125	127	129	129	132	128	125

2. PAYMENT-BY-RESULTS WORKERS

Classes of workers	1963	1964	1965	1966	1967	1968	1969	1970	1971	1972	1973	1974	1975
Fitters (Skilled—other than toolroom and maintenance)	144	146	147	150	154	151	151	148	148	147	142	136	130
Turners and machinemen (other than toolroom and maintenance)													
—rated at or above fitter's rate	145	146	147	147	150	148	150	148	148	148	143	138	133
—rated below fitter's rate	134	137	138	138	137	137	139	135	139	138	133	129	124
Toolroom fitters and turners	146	149	150	152	154	155	153	150	151	149	147	140	136
Maintenance men (skilled)													
—skilled maintenance fitters	133	134	136	137	140	140	139	139	147	143	137	131	132
—skilled maintenance electricians	136	137	137	138	140	142	143	143	149	145	141	132	134
—other skilled maintenance classes	130	132	133	135	138	135	135	138	140	138	133	127	125
Patternmakers	141	140	139	142	146	142	145	144	144	143	137	132	127
Sheet metal workers (skilled)	156	161	157	159	162	164	166	160	160	156	151	147	134
Moulders (loose pattern-skilled)	144	148	145	147	150	148	147	143	141	138	139	135	130
Platers, riveters, caulkers	143	142	142	144	146	144	143	141	144	140	134	129	135
All skilled grades	146	147	148	150	152	150	151	148	149	148	143	137	132
All semi-skilled grades	134	137	137	136	136	136	135	133	135	131	127	122	119

1 Excluding Overtime Premium. Measured in June of each year.

Source: Department of Employment.

Table B

Average Hourly Earnings of Skilled Male Workers as a Percentage of those for Labourers in Selected Engineering Industries *

	Timeworkers				Payments-By-Results Workers			
	1963	1967	1971	1975	1963	1967	1971	1975
Mechanical Engineering								
Skilled	39.9	42.3	39.1	28.3	43.1	47.2	44.2	28.3
Semi-skilled	15.0	17.4	17.9	16.4	24.8	24.4	24.7	16.5
Electrical Engineering								
Skilled	44.6	46.3	44.3	34.6	39.8	43.8	39.6	33.4
Semi-skilled	15.6	18.4	19.6	17.0	21.7	23.1	25.0	19.4
Motor Vehicle Manufacturing								
Skilled	43.9	46.4	44.8	27.8	63.7	66.0	52.6	31.3
Semi-skilled	33.0	20.7	29.3	22.6	58.7	61.2	40.7	23.7
Aerospace Equipment Manufacturing & Repairing								
Skilled	58.3	52.8	58.6	38.6	57.3	61.4	43.2	43.0
Semi-skilled	20.9	14.4	21.3	14.7	27.0	27.0	19.8	23.9

* Measured in June of each year and excluding overtime premium.

Source: Department of Employment

Table C

Average Hourly Earnings of Skilled Male Workers as a Percentage of those for Semi-Skilled Workers in Selected Engineering Industries *

	Timeworkers				Payment-by-results Workers			
	1963	1967	1971	1975	1963	1967	1971	1975
Mechanical Engineering	21.7	21.2	18.0	10.3	14.7	18.3	15.6	10.2
Electrical Engineering	25.1	23.6	20.7	15.1	14.9	16.8	11.7	11.7
Motor Vehicle Manufacturing	8.2	21.3	12.0	4.2	3.2	3.0	8.5	6.1
Aerospace equipment Manufacturing & repairing	30.9	33.6	30.8	20.8	23.9	27.1	19.5	15.4

* Measured in June of each year. Excludes overtime premium.

Source: Department of Employment

Table D

Average Percentage Hourly Earnings Differentials: *
Skilled Adult Male Workers in Selected Engineering Occupations and Industries over Labourers

1. TIMEWORKERS

Classes of workers	Mechanical Engineering		Electrical Engineering		Aerospace etc		Motor Vehicles, etc		All Engineering	
	1970	1975	1970	1975	1970	1975	1970	1975	1970	1975
Fitters (Skilled—other than toolroom and maintenance)	33	23	42	34	47	38	48	27	39	28
Turners and machinemen (other than toolroom and maintenance)										
—rated at or above fitter's rate	37	26	48	39	57	47	51	28	39	31
—rated below fitter's rate	23	16	22	21	24	19	44	26	24	22
Toolroom fitters and turners	51	35	60	45	63	41	53	31	58	38
Maintenance men (skilled)										
—skilled maintenance fitters	40	33	45	36	45	36	44	27	43	33
—skilled maintenance electricians	44	34	41	40	51	38	50	34	48	38
—other skilled maintenance classes	33	28	36	35	45	33	47	31	44	34
Patternmakers	41	30	49	40	57	29	50	27	50	34
Sheet metal workers (skilled)	37	27	34	24	58	40	42	28	38	26
Moulders (loose pattern-skilled)	37	18	52	—	—	—	—	—	31	18
Platers, riveters, caulkers	36	32	30	30	—	—	—	—	42	31
All skilled grades	38	28	42	35	54	38	47	28	44	32

2. PAYMENT-BY-RESULTS WORKERS

Classes of workers	Mechanical Engineering		Electrical Engineering		Aerospace, etc		Motor Vehicles, etc		All Engineering	
	1970	1975	1970	1975	1970	1975	1970	1975	1970	1975
Fitters (Skilled—other than toolroom and maintenance)	46	28	39	30	52	39	60	28	48	30
Turners and machinemen (other than toolroom and maintenance)										
—rated at or above fitter's rate	46	30	42	30	62	52	52	36	48	33
—rated below fitter's rate	30	19	28	25	31	32	41	30	35	24
Toolroom fitters and turners	50	35	47	38	52	48	53	40	50	36
Maintenance men (skilled)										
—skilled maintenance fitters	39	28	41	53	48	40	34	20	39	32
—skilled maintenance electricians	43	28	43	59	—	38	47	30	43	34
—other skilled maintenance classes	39	23	36	28	48	36	29	—	38	25
Patternmakers	44	21	57	35	66	49	46	—	44	27
Sheet metal workers (skilled)	46	29	37	27	68	42	58	35	60	34
Moulders (loose pattern-skilled)	47	30	51	25	—	—	—	—	43	30
Platers, riveters, caulkers	48	35	54	16	—	—	30	—	41	35
All skilled grades	45	28	39	33	56	43	52	31	48	32

* Excluding Overtime Premium. Measured in June of each year.

Source: Department of Employment

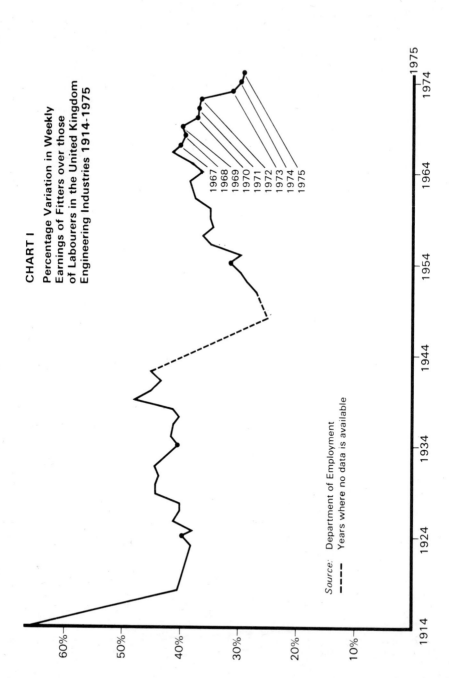

CHART I

Percentage Variation in Weekly
Earnings of Fitters over those
of Labourers in the United Kingdom
Engineering Industries 1914-1975

Source: Department of Employment
- - - - Years where no data is available

IV   Manpower Planning and Apprentice Training

The Engineering Industry Training Board's Annual Report regularly refers to the strange propensity of the industry to take on apprentices in boom times and reduce the intake at the bottom of the cycle. This short-sighted policy has often been commented upon by trade unions and employers' associations, and not least by those companies who have pursued such policies and who in consequence will have few, if any, skilled people coming through the system over the next two or three years. This once again produces a situation where you set about robbing Peter to pay Paul, where one company strips the skilled assets of another to make up its own deficiencies. In 1974 there was an increased intake in comparison with 1973, but this was only achieved after companies had introduced more active recruitment policies. In fact, some companies only achieved their 1974 figures by lowering recruitment standards. Many companies have stepped up contacts with schools, and many of them complain that school careers officers know little about engineering. I have found this to be particularly so, and it is most disheartening to speak to some careers officers when trying to persuade them to guide young people into industry. On this particular matter one can take some encouragement from the fact that an 'Engineering Careers Information Service' has been set up. This is being jointly sponsored by the Engineering Employers' Federation, the Confederation of Shipbuilding and Engineering Unions (CSEU) and the Engineering Industry Training Board (EITB). The aim of this service is to inform young people still at school, school leavers and those at college or university about the industry and the career opportunities it offers.

Traditionally the major method of entry to various skilled jobs has been through craft apprenticeships, entering on leaving school at about the age of 16 years. Although an increasing number of workers is obtaining skills through up-grading and training within companies, such training rarely provides a skill transferable between different employers such as that acquired through a craft apprenticeship. It therefore follows, even with all its shortcomings, that the apprenticeship system will continue to provide the majority of craftsmen for many years to come.

It is perhaps worth examining the shortcomings of the present system and the long-term effects they will have on the industry. In the period 1965/66 to 1973/74 there has been a decline not only in the total number of employees and craftsmen in the engineering industry but also a proportionate decline in the number of craftsmen as a percentage of the total labour force in the industry from 21 to 18%. The decline in the total number employed in the industry reflected the general trend in the UK of the decrease in the numbers in manufacturing employment.

These alterations in the structure of the labour force focus attention on the flows into and out of the industry. On the recruitment side there has been a drastic decline in the number of engineering craftsmen and technician trainees entering the industry, particularly for the period 1971 to 1974, bringing further problems of shortages for 1976/78. The situation is best illustrated by the following figures, which show that the number of first-year engineering craft and technician trainees has moved from 24,000 in 1966/67 to 27,200 in 1968/69, 19,500 in 1971/72, 15,250 in 1972/73 and 22,000 in 1975/76. The EITB supplemented recruitment by means of a Training Award Scheme for school leavers by 2,500 in 1971/72, 1,500 in 1972/73 and 4,000 in 1975/76. This scheme was introduced by the EITB because of poor recruitment by the industry, and these apprentices were actually employed by the EITB during the course of their first year of training. The Board endeavoured during this period to find them employment within engineering, with a considerable degree of success. According to the EITB, the net loss during training is perhaps 25 to 30% of the original number of craft recruits.

The basic problem is that taking into account the trainees opting out, the industry requires an annual intake of 25,000 to 27,000 recruits a year simply to replace those lost by retirement, promotion or those leaving it. Table 1 on page 6 illustrates the increasing ratios of apprentices to skilled men (1:6.4 in 1964 compared with 1:9.5 in 1974).

The question of apprentices' pay was discussed with employers to see if one could correlate reluctance to train with that of pay levels. From the limited amount of evidence available, it was clear that there was some doubt about the reasons for any shortfall in demand for apprenticeship places, but two points which recurred were the aspects of apprentices' pay, and differentials between apprentices and non-trainees as mentioned previously.

Summary and Conclusions

This paper has examined the nature of the skilled labour shortage and the way some companies have endeavoured to devise policies in order to maximise the available supply of skilled labour.

The United Kingdom engineering industry has been declining in its competitive position in the world and its productivity too has been disappointing. Employment has decreased from a peak of 4.4 million in 1966 to 3.8 million in 1974 and the number of skilled men involved has been falling too. But what is probably most significant is that the ratio of apprentices to skilled workers is now 9.5 compared with 6.4 in 1964. At the same time, British industrialists continue to indicate that skilled labour shortages are an important impediment to increased output. By tradition, the immediate response of engineering employers in any shortage situation is to try to recruit from the external labour markets, when in fact a supply of skilled labour is very often present in the company. There is a wastage problem caused by job dissatisfaction which can be resolved by changes in individual company policies. Factors which contribute to the skilled man's dissatisfaction include insecurity, erosion of differentials, lack of status, poor working conditions, and an unsatisfactory industrial relations climate. It is necessary though, to state that working conditions and industrial relations do not figure highly in the reasons given by skilled men for leaving the industry, and to counteract these problems it is suggested that companies adopt job enrichment policies. However, most skilled men reject this solution as being irrelevant to their main problems.

The paper suggests that security of employment is uppermost amongst demands and that a company's failure to provide it can have an important bearing on its capacity to gain agreements, to change policies, and thus to retain skilled labour. This is mainly due to the effects of the business cycle, from which the engineering industry appears to have suffered more than most. Job security is clearly important, but not the sole consideration.

Many people complain about unsatisfactory levels and structures of earnings and methods of pay. Ample evidence exists to show that relative pay levels in the industry, and for craftsmen within it, are narrowing. There are also examples of wage increases reversing a shortage problem, although this practice is now very much restricted by incomes restraint policies. There has been a series of internal disputes on the question of representation for skilled men at one company for over two years. Their aspiration is to be able to represent themselves independently from production workers and therefore have a greater influence on the type of wage claims being presented to the company. Since 1969, flat, across-the-board increases were negotiated, with the result that the differential between a skilled and unskilled worker had been eroded by about 12%. What was once an appropriate wage structure has now become quite the opposite. Further evidence shows that the direct effects of inappropriate wage structures are causing dissatisfaction, particularly among the younger generation.

There is an increasing demand for recognition of status, to which some trade unionists and managements have not yet become attuned. This recognition takes the form of staff status and conditions and causes many problems for both workers and management. In some cases the staff wage structure is no better than that of manual workers, although there are the advantages of sickness and pension schemes. However, difficulties for management arise if they concede staff status to skilled men in isolation.

When examining the differences between staff and manual worker conditions, strong evidence shows that some degree of harmonisation has taken place particularly on conditions such as hours of work, holidays, and other fringe benefits. However, it was suggested by some employers that this issue of 'second class employees' is one with which many companies are financially ill-equipped to cope; consequently, more skilled men will inevitably be lost to the industry, particularly among the young, where status is becoming increasingly important.

When considering the shortage of skilled labour, it is necessary to examine the apprentice recruitment policies of companies, and it appears that most companies are experiencing a continuing decline in the number of applicants despite special recruitment drives. Scope exists for considerable debate and examination of the underlying causes and long-term significance of the decrease in the numbers and proportions of apprenticeships in any sector.

Whether the trends are of longer term significance depends on the view taken of the influence of such factors as technological change, and the proper utilisation of skilled manpower, on the demand for people with various levels of skill. While statistics of notified vacancies and registered unemployment suggest frequent shortages of labour in some skills, there is evidence that technological change, particularly in engineering, is leading to increased demand for technicians and semi-skilled people. Whatever view is taken on these longer term issues, demographic trends, changes in the educational system, and economic conditions combined in the early 1970s to reduce the number of apprentices in many areas. This will undoubtedly influence the numbers of newly qualified skilled men in the period 1976 to 1978.

The cry from government and industry where there is a perceived shortage is 'more training'. This may be described as the bathplug effect. You pull out the plug and at the same time turn on the tap to keep up the level of water. Unfortunately a lot of water goes down the drain, never to return. In spite of all the financial assistance now available, the fact is that it still costs companies thousands of pounds to train one skilled man: it is therefore a colossal waste of time and money when they do not use their expertise. This is particularly disturbing when one considers the type of occupations some skilled men take up. A recent NEDO survey of engineers and patternmakers who had left the industry showed that many of the skills acquired were still being used, but many had taken up such occupations as insurance agents, gas meter readers, mobile bread salesmen. Taking a cynical view, two ex-toolmakers took up useful occupations, one became a whisky blender and the other a grave digger!

Reference has been made to the anti-industry bias of our education system, which I consider to be relevant. It is a deep and fundamental problem, covering many occupations and going beyond the skilled workers' area into the echelons of management. Production managers and production engineers are two examples where recruitment for courses in these two professions is derisory. Education for industry and production management is an interrelated area which in my opinion is worthy of further detailed examination.

Finally, the industry desperately needs to improve its image not only to retain its existing skilled workers but also to have a beneficial effect on recruitment. It is also necessary for society to recognise that the foreman, the draughtsman, and the toolmaker are making a greater contribution to our economic well-being than many more modish and prestigious employments.

Is it too much to hope that eventually the element of our educational system that guides young people away from pro-ductive industry will change its mind and divert its pupils in the direction of engineering and manufacturing? Can the tide be turned? Can the country begin to understand that an efficient and profitable engineering and manufacturing industry is the essential base on which to build a prosperous and compassionate society? I believe it can, but it needs the complete understanding and co-operation of government, trade unions, employers and educationalists.

Members of the British-North American Committee

Chairmen
NICHOLAS J. CAMPBELL, JR.
Director and Senior Vice President,
Exxon Corporation, New York

SIR RICHARD DOBSON
President, British-American Tobacco Co
Ltd., and Chairman, British Leyland
Ltd., London

Vice Chairman
IAN MacGREGOR
Chairman, AMAX Incorporated,
Greenwich, Connecticut

Chairman, Executive Committee
W. O. TWAITS
Director and Vice President,
Royal Bank of Canada,
Toronto, Canada

Members
A. ROBERT ABBOUD
Deputy Chairman of the Board,
The First National Bank of Chicago,
Chicago, Illinois

JAMES G. AFFLECK
Chairman and President,
American Cyanamid Company,
Wayne, New Jersey

W. S. ANDERSON
Chairman and President,
NCR Corporation, Dayton, Ohio

ERNEST C. ARBUCKLE
Chairman, Wells Fargo Bank,
San Francisco, California

J. A. ARMSTRONG
Chairman and Chief Executive Officer,
Imperial Oil Limited,
Toronto, Ontario

A. E. BALLOCH
Executive Vice President,
Bowater Incorporated,
Old Greenwich, Connecticut

SIR DAVID BARRAN
A Managing Director, Shell Transport
and Trading Co Ltd., London

SIR DONALD BARRON
Group Chairman,
Rowntree Mackintosh Ltd., York

DAVID BASNETT
General Secretary, General and
Municipal Workers' Union,
Esher, Surrey

ROBERT BELGRAVE
Planning Adviser,
British Petroleum Limited, London

C. FRED BERGSTEN
Senior Fellow, The Brookings
Institution, Washington D.C.

I. H. STUART BLACK
Chairman, General Accident Fire and
Life Assurance Corporation Ltd.,
Perth, Scotland

HOWARD BLAUVELT
Chairman and Chief Executive Officer,
Continental Oil Company,
Stamford, Connecticut

* JOHN F. BOOKOUT
President, Shell Oil Co.,
Houston, Texas

JOHN F. BURLINGAME
Vice President and Group Executive,
International and Canadian Group
General Electric Company,
Fairfield, Connecticut

DR. CHARLES CARTER
Vice Chancellor,
University of Lancaster, Lancaster

SILAS S. CATHCART
Chairman and Chief Executive Officer,
Illinois Tool Works Inc.,
Chicago, Illinois

SIR FREDERICK CATHERWOOD
Director, John Laing and Son Limited,
London

HAROLD van B. CLEVELAND
Vice President, First National City Bank,
New York

KIT COPE
Overseas Director, Confederation of
British Industry, London

* DIRK DE BRUYNE
Managing Director, Royal Dutch/Shell
Group of Companies, London

WILLIAM DODGE
Ottawa, Ontario

ALASTAIR F. DOWN
Chairman and Chief Executive,
Burmah Oil Company, Swindon

GERRY EASTWOOD
General Secretary, Association of
Patternmakers and Allied Craftsmen,
London

H. E. EKBLOM
Chairman, European American Bank,
New York

ix

XI

Sponsoring Organisations

The British-North American Research Association was inaugurated in December 1969. Its primary purpose is to sponsor research on British-North American economic relations in association with the British-North American Committee. Publications of the British-North American Research Association as well as publications of the British-North American Committee are available at the Association's office, 1 Gough Square, London EC4, (Tel. 01-353 6371). The Association is recognised as a charity and is governed by a Council under the chairmanship of Sir Richard Dobson.

The National Planning Association was founded in 1934 as an independent, private, non-profit, and non-political organisation. It engages in studies and develops recommendations based on non-partisan research or analysis on major policy issues confronting the United States, both in domestic affairs and in international relations. Its research provides information and methodologies valuable to public and private decision makers.

NPA is governed by a Board of Trustees representing all private sectors of the American economy—business, labour, farm, and the professions. The Executive Committee of the Board, the five Standing Committees (the Agriculture, Business and Labour Committees on National Policy, the National Committee on America's Goals and Resources, and the Committee on International Policy), and special Policy Committees (including the British-North American Committee) originate and approve policy statements and reports. Major research projects undertaken for government and international agencies, and through foundation grants, are carried out with the guidance of research advisory committees providing the best knowledge available. The full-time staff of the Association totals around 80 professional and administrative personnel.

The Association has a public membership of some 2,000 individuals, corporations, organisations, and groups. NPA activities are financed by contributions from individuals, business firms, trade unions, and farm organisations; by grants for specific research projects from private foundations; and by research contracts with federal, state and local government agencies and international organisations.

NPA publications, including those of the British-North American Committee, can be obtained from the Association's office, 1606 New Hampshire Avenue, N.W., Washington, D.C. 20009 (Tel. 202-265-7685).

The C.D. Howe Research Institute is a private, non-political, non-profit organisation founded in January 1973, by the merger of the C.D. Howe Memorial Foundation and the Private Planning Association of Canada (PPAC), to undertake research into Canadian economic policy issues, especially in the areas of international policy and major government programmes.

HRI continues the activities of the PPAC. These include the work of three established committees, composed of agricultural, business, educational, labour, and professional leaders. The committees are the Canadian Economic Policy Committee, which has been concentrating on Canadian economic issues, especially in the area of trade, since 1961; the Canadian-American Committee, which has dealt with relations between Canada and the United States since 1957 and is jointly sponsored by HRI and the National Planning Association in Washington; and the British-North American Committee, formed in 1969 and sponsored jointly by the National Planning Association, the British-North American Research Association in London, and HRI. Each of the committees meets twice a year to consider important current issues and to sponsor and review studies that contribute to better public understanding of such issues.

In addition to taking over the publications of the three PPAC committees, HRI releases the work of its staff, and occasionally of outside authors, in four other publications: *Observations,* six or seven of which are published each year; *Policy Review and Outlook,* published annually; *Special Studies,* to provide detailed analysis of major policy issues for publication on an occasional basis; and *Commentaries,* to give wide circulation to the views of experts on issues of current Canadian interest.

HRI publications, including those of the British-North American Committee, are available from the Institute's offices, 2064 Sun Life Building, Montreal, Quebec H3B 2X7 (Tel. 514-879-1254).